Prayeretry

Prayeretry

At the Feet of Jesus

Shelly Boggs

RESOURCE *Publications* • Eugene, Oregon

PRAYERETRY
At the Feet of Jesus

Copyright © 2021 Shelly Boggs. All rights reserved. Except for brief quotations in critical publications or reviews, no part of this book may be reproduced in any manner without prior written permission from the publisher. Write: Permissions, Wipf and Stock Publishers, 199 W. 8th Ave., Suite 3, Eugene, OR 97401.

Resource Publications
An Imprint of Wipf and Stock Publishers
199 W. 8th Ave., Suite 3
Eugene, OR 97401

www.wipfandstock.com

PAPERBACK ISBN: 978-1-6667-3111-8
HARDCOVER ISBN: 978-1-6667-2456-1
EBOOK ISBN: 978-1-6667-2457-8

10/28/21

To my husband, David, my heartbeat; my children, Keelie, Michael and Jason—my delight, my pride and joy, and my jubilation. To my bonus daughters, Ila and Rachel. Thank you for loving my sons so well. To my niece and kindred spirit, Jessica. And to my grandchildren, Bryant, Nevaeh, Maverick, Ellie, and Zoey. You make my heart full to overflowing.

Contents

Preface | ix

Alpha and Omega | 1
What was it Like | 3
Amaze | 5
The Armor of God | 7
Battle Cry of an Overcomer | 9
Refinement | 12
A Day at the Beach | 14
Burgundy | 16
Intentional Devotion | 18
Posterity | 19
Under His Wing | 22
The Cool of the Day | 24
Roman Road | 25
The Calling | 27

Harvest | 28
Paradise | 29
Quantify | 32
The Touch | 33
Peace be Still | 35
Breathe | 37
And There is Praise | 39
Strength in the Light | 41
For His Purpose | 43
Growing | 45
The Revelation | 47

Appendix: Scripture References and Inspirational Scripture | 49
Bibliography | 65

Preface

I FINALLY CAME TO terms with the fact I was a mess, not only in need of emotional healing but physical healing, as well. I often questioned the Lord why I had to go down this path, not at all of my choosing. It was very confusing. What possible good could ever come from any of it? I had a strange connection with heartache and despair. I knew total humiliation; I knew betrayal, and I knew brokenness. However, my God was and is bigger than any of this. He is a God of love, restoration, and redemption. At the very beginning of this situation, as clear as a bell, I heard the Lord say, *"This is going to be an uphill battle, but you hold your head up."*

Still trying to make some sense of the ordeal, a few years ago, I made it a personal goal to read my favorite Bible from cover to cover. Reading a Bible from cover to cover was nothing new to me. I have had a structured Bible reading program for over thirty-five years. However, this time was different. It was not a race, but an in-depth study, letting my mind and spirit be saturated and filled by the Word. This included all the chapters, every article, and every footnote; no matter how long it took for the hunger and thirst to be satisfied. My approach was to be totally receptive and open to what the Lord had for me. Looking back, I see this was the instrument God used to do a mighty work in me regarding the healing for which I was so desperate.

Preface

Fortunately, while going through such difficulties and struggles, I had a great support group in a loving family and church family. I will never forget how encouraging my pastor, Bruce McCarty, was during this most difficult time in my life. He and his wife, Janet, have been such a blessing to our family, and our church. Their stewardship has been unwavering. I thank the Lord for sending us to Owasso First Assembly more than twenty-five years prior.

About two-thirds into this Bible reading endeavor, Bible in one hand, pad, and pencil in the other, I began taking notes of what the Holy Spirit would say to me. As I studied a particular topic, the Lord revealed to me the poetic possibilities. This process began around June 2018 and continued through March 2021. It was then I realized the collection of poems could be a book. As each poem was written I noted in an Appendix section, the scripture that had inspired the thought or verse. I then discovered the book could also be used as a Bible Study.

I now understand if I had never gone down the difficult paths the Lord allowed, I never would have written this book. I hope your spirit is encouraged and uplifted. Please enjoy *Prayeretry*.

Alpha and Omega

In the beginning, yet You were there,
no form or space in the atmosphere

You spoke into darkness and called in the light,
divided the heavens with words of Your might

Then spoke out to time and set it in motion
Dryland arose, lush clear to the ocean

Wonders were formed in the heavens to view
Next, creatures large and small made their debut

You said, let Us make in Our image, the man
and so, life as we know it began

He will be special with spirit and soul
We will give him capacity for love and emotion, but will not control

The first one will fail for the gap will be wide,
for sin was acknowledged and judgment applied

Atonement is lacking, the price is the Son
The gap must be bridged, and so it was done

Offering salvation, forgiveness, and hope, he came
His only requirement, accept him and live for him without shame

Upheaval, hatred, and jealousy threatened leadership of the day
They plotted to arrest him and kill him without delay

Tormented, beaten, bruised, and alone—
the stone the builders rejected is the foundation and chief cornerstone

And so is the journey; a path must be chosen from within
I AM the beginning and the end. Come, Lord Jesus, his grace be with us all. Amen

What was it Like

What was it like when God turned away,
when You bore my sin and endured such pain?

How could You hold the sins of the earth,
withstand the torment, ridicule, scoffing, and hurt?

When You cried out to God finishing what You started,
was it at that time Satan realized his plans were thwarted?

When the Father again held Your gaze,
were You watching the veil tear with loving amaze?

Willingly Heaven's Lamb and humanity's all,
completely enough for Adam's fall

Did the east and the west collide that day,
forever taking my sins each way?

Did the abyss jump up and catch my sin,
or did he moan and groan all from within?

Could You feel heaven's countenance fall in haste,
building the bridge of mercy and grace?

Did You descend in a flash snatching those keys,
or bide Your time with stride and ease?

Could You hear the demons screeching and screaming,
or see their defeat collectively seething?

Could hell hear heaven's triumphant jubilation?
Perhaps it was heard in every constellation

Answers to these will one day be known—
that wonderful day when love brings me home

Amaze

Abundantly and cleverly, You continue to amaze
Brilliantly, unselfishly, unequivocally, You shower love and grace

Please . . . stay with me in this quiet place a little longer
Build my faith, encourage me and make me stronger

Though I know that when I go You go before me
You, above all, see the condition of this world ever so clearly

Turmoil spinning all around,
hatred spewing far and loud

People doing selfish things,
even though havoc it always brings

If we could all adhere to Your great command,
we would see a world You had originally planned

No more wars or genocides or hate
If we would love You above all, our neighbor we would appreciate

But I know that everything is in alignment according to Your will
Deep within my soul, You tell me to *"Know and to be still"*

Listening, I acknowledge the truth of Your Holy Word
Lifting my eyes to You my spirit within is stirred

Though confusion hovers in the air,
I will trust, draw near, and will not despair

I honor and praise You, my God, and my salvation—
a mighty majesty to be adored from generation to generation

I sing praises to You, my God, who parts the waters and makes a way
I sing praises to You, my God, who lovingly cares for me each day

Might I ask . . . oh, hear my plea . . . may we see beauty beyond the haze
For abundantly and cleverly You continue to amaze

The Armor of God

Weapons rising have fallen away
Evil's schemes impenetrable through my shield today

My confidence and victories are secure,
it is all in my Savior's name that I AM sure

Though evil knocks to devour my flesh,
I close the door, and in my Lord, I AM refreshed

I recognize the battleground, in him, I must claim
Not by my power but by the power of his Holy Name

Choosing my armor, I remember it wisely,
for in his Word, it is scripted precisely

Being surrounded by knowledge of the truth is my fate
His righteousness guards my heart as a breastplate

My feet stand firm in the gospel of peace
I AM shielded by faith uttering prayers that never cease

My mind protected and confident in a helmet of salvation
For I am a citizen of God's holy nation

My weapon of choice, my trustworthy sword—
the infallible transcription of God's Holy Word

In prayer, I persevere as a good soldier should,
though evil flings turmoil, solid ground is withstood

Strongholds are conquered in captivating thought,
Godly character, purity, and integrity are sought

I know my enemy and am aware of his tactics—
he is a liar, a thief, a destroyer; he is evil and it's all just semantics

I fill my mind with kingdom thoughts and of my Savior's saving grace,
I proclaim his promises, authority, pray in the Spirit, and give him praise

Battle Cry of an Overcomer

Still a child really, experiencing life's wrath,
You called me from my wayward path

Unworthy, untrusting, relying on self,
gradually and steadily, You pursued my wealth

Intervening on my behalf; the number You alone know,
instructing me, guiding me, challenging me to grow

You gave me purpose and clear direction,
though not without challenges and much correction

Blessing and favor You did not withhold,
increasing my territory, broadening my role

Retirement ahead of which I did plan,
So looking forward to time with my clan

A good rapport I had garnered with tenure,
but I was looking forward to my next adventure

Nearly three decades I was assigned there,
the last year my spirit in much despair

In public, the evil one waged war with my soul,
a reputation in question, an emotional toll

Lies and half-truths twisted to discredit
En masse the frenzy all without merit

Signed agreements no longer had meaning,
political moves all in the teaming

Confusion piercing, doubt prevailing,
one truth unwavering, Your love unfailing

So-called friends falling away,
betrayal and heartbreak among the array

My honor and value in a downward spiral,
integrity and worthiness presumably on trial

An uphill battle, You said it would be,
but I was assured You would never leave me

The attack advancing from the left and the right,
my instruction was to *be still* and let You fight

But Lord, they're saying I did thus and so
Does it really matter, as long as I know?

To be wrongfully accused in public display
Of course, You would know. Forgive me, I'm feeling selfish today

Give me strength and help me not care what another believes
Little one, I understand, remember they hung Me with thieves

Pray for each one intending you harm
I can't; I won't; but then I repented in alarm

Blessing and favor to them I did pray
Awareness and truth of Your Spirit I laid

Hours on end spending time in Your Word
Scripture speaking and repairing what had occurred

Recognizing my enemy in Your Name called him out,
I am a child of the Most High God, I continued to shout

Peace and assurance hid me under Your wing
In praise and worship, I daily did sing

Lord, spare me all anguish and make something good
To light bring the truth, I plead that you would

One-third of a year was consumed with this plight
Over two hundred scriptures I proclaimed each day and night

Family and friends sending prayer I could feel
ALAS, the bindings were broken, and the truth revealed

Praise be to God and power and dominion—
this daughter is grateful beyond comprehension!

Refinement

Hear my prayer, O God, as I call upon Your name
Use trials for my benefit and growth, in the name of Jesus, I proclaim

Help me not succumb, or even cope, but victoriously persevere
With humility, I beseech You and ask for wisdom sincere

Draw me to listen and actively seek Your will
Put me on a path called straight; a mind of Christ would You instill

Give me compassion for others and authority over my tongue,
seeking Your face, hating evil; an anthem to be sung

Bestow in me unnatural patience while awaiting You to move,
establish the work of my hands, Lord, as I begin anew

Render in me virtue and when I am troubled call me to pray
Whether sick in body, mind, spirit, or nation, need for You let me earnestly convey

By Your Spirit let me flee from sin and for others carry burdens to be healed
For by Your blood, I am righteous and the attention of the Almighty I shall wield

In obedience, let me go wherever You lead, even if in search of
    only one
By my weakness let me be strong with the consuming power of
    the Son

Sustain me with an unwavering ability to endure,
whether in sickness, suffering, or extreme difficulty, my trust in
    You I procure

Though I may not understand, I know You are working things
    out for the good
Abundant example testifies of hardships Your people have
    withstood

Instill in me, Lord, a reverence for You I will never take for
    granted
Till the ground removing the weeds and in fertile soil let me be
    firmly planted

Call me to a higher place; let me be the best that I can be
When the dross burns away and the reflection looks back, let it be
    You they see, not me

A Day at the Beach
For David, unto the Lord

Deep blue hues of ocean ripples, I see; I am mesmerized by Your creation
White sands adorning the scene—a somber reminder of adoration

Peace and serenity softly crash as the waves appear and recede
A family of porpoises teases the air as they playfully proceed

The blue cloudless sky and the distant water afar blend to the horizon beyond,
in this solace I feel Your presence and am overwhelmingly calmed

An old woman strolls along looking for the seas' discarded treasures,
and a young woman watches her pace that she continually measures

A middle-aged man casts his line out to the breaking waves,
an old man offers his advice—a skill in which he raves

Two ships fill the void in the open waters' distance,
acknowledging the space between them, they pass with no resistance

From the east I see my love returning from an afar pier
He is the one that You gave me, the one that I endear

As he approaches, I feel so blessed thinking of our journey
    together,
whether exploring or quietly at home, quality time is a pleasure

Over three decades and four we have navigated this life,
I gratefully think of the family we have raised and am marveled
    You picked me for his wife

How the future unfolds as we age, I wonder at times,
but I know we shall trust and rest in assurance, for the future is in
    Your designs

Burgundy

The most valuable substance from the beginning of time,
yet the capacity of worth that day completely sublime

Piercing, premeditated measures yielded the depths to which the enticers fell,
pooling on the ground it lay descending into hell

Who could have known and who would have thought,
the price at which it had been bought?

While in the body it coursed through his veins,
a mystery to the universe the wise would never explain

Piety housed the lacerated flesh as it fell from the bone
Generation upon generation did this wine humbly and willingly atone

The hosts of heaven grievously watched as each drop poured out and spilled,
onlookers mostly cheering for more, as the Savior gave of his own free will

A channel to God lay on the ground reflecting on the Son
A ransom was paid for all souls the devil thought he had won

A promise fulfilled as open wounds cleansed and purified each repentant sinner

In just a few days this would be made known to the ultimate condemner

The mercy seat of God beaten and bleeding upon an everlasting Ark,
a sacrifice made for all mankind for a world so broken and dark

No greater love was ever shown nor ever a heart so pure
Of all the majesties of the world, this One we can be sure

Justification, sanctification, and forgiveness offered each time a drop would fall,
the saving grace of the *blood*—offered once and for all

Intentional Devotion

Thank You for all the blessings, Lord; let us intimately know Your heart
Let us be grounded in Your Word before each day that we start

Protect us from evil influence so prevalent in this world
Let us know when we are pulling away from You and not moving toward

Give us exceptional character and understanding of You,
renewing our hearts and minds to be true

Let us know Your will for our lives
Let us be strong and courageous choosing love over strife

Remind us often of Your diligent care
Help us be good examples; for others' burdens we are to bear

May the knowledge of You continually be expressed
Let us have love and compassion for the spiritually oppressed

Posterity

Scanning the globe high and low, even through trials,
I know of no better place than the USA and am convinced there
is no denial

Though the people's tranquility and common defense, to some,
supposedly obscured
In addition, it has been said, justice and welfare are unsecured

Shadows of a dream reflect explosive emotions so intense
How will we come together and what is the price of recompense?

Persons standing trial for breaking the law must be impartially
judged,
for a democracy to properly function, of this we cannot budge

Social issues of the day seem to bog down the first responders
How could this be improved? Is this something to ponder?

Those who use their position of authority to oppress—let the
entitlement be gone,
replace it, Lord, with grace and love, and unto You let all be
drawn

Wounds so deep birthed hatred before the circle of the stars
Blood red stripes on fields of white, generationally marred

The answers are only in You, God. Search our hearts and in pure faith teach us how to pray
Let this crossroad be a responsibility; let it be so Lord, without delay

Protect those, O God, who are securing our peace and quality of life
Let everyone take a deep breath, attain perspective, and put away the strife

The echo of King George III, reminders of battles for freedom already fought
Have we learned anything from history or was it all for naught?

If we must see color, let it not be color of the skin,
rather, the beauty and individuality of the person from within

Of the people, by the people, and for the people, again decreed let one and all be free,
indivisible, through four bloody years, said let it be

When is enough, enough, many say one to another?
Complacency has been a problem, it seems, instead of love for our brother

I'm not looking at this predicament through glasses the color of rose
People from every walk of life will need help with the challenges before us, I suppose

O Lord God, encourage those who step into harm's way for us each day,
their importance and respect, let us not betray

In humbleness, we ask You Lord, shed Your grace, once more
Crown us again with brotherhood stretching from shore to shore

O God, how we need on our behalf, for You to move
Open our hearts and minds to repentance; the strongholds please reprove

For the land of the free and home of the brave, In God, we trust and exclaim—
One nation, under God, we proclaim

Under His Wing

I recognize the one who draws first blood; the one who longs to make the cut
He waits and calculates; it is not happenstance, anything but

Waiting to insert the blade precisely when my back is turned
He strategically plans the attack; of my well-being, he is not concerned

He may be planning to rally forces intent on cutting me to the quick,
would even love to give me one good, stern, and poignant kick

He spews his venom and his lies
Watches in the shadows of his web; a clearly ingenious disguise

Oh, how intimidated he must be and full of hate
He patiently waits; the encounter not left to fate

For an encore, rains down confusion then initiates the offense
I am clothed in my armor; let the battle commence

I may feel an infliction and possibly carry a wound deeply
I may be battered and bruised, but not destroyed completely

Unlikely though, the evil one has forgotten with whom he is dealing
God Almighty is my protector, and it is to him the Devil will be kneeling

Satan may think me intimidated; he'll be happy with any imposed distress
However, my Lord will rescue me from all who intend to harm and oppress

Whatever the planned device, be it pain, sickness, or simply deflating my sail,
I recognize the source, so the siege will fail

I will count it all joy whatever upheaval may scatter
Whatever the method, it really doesn't matter

Refreshed and renewed, my Lord will raise me up, and he will make me strong
It is he who comes to my rescue and to him whom I belong

By the name of Jesus, I proclaim authority over all affliction, and unto him, I will cling
For when the war is raging, it is Jesus who will fight, while I am tucked securely under His wing

I may falter and I may stumble
But to get to me, the enemy must go through Jesus—who will make evil tremble!

The Cool of the Day

Will You meet me in the cool of the day?
I long to reveal my heart along the way

Guide me and consume me from within
Teach me Your ways; with the world I'll not contend

The conversation lingers in this quiet place,
through the casting of my cares, I am running my race

In You, I am refreshed and my spirit is renewed
I come to Your table; there is nothing You exclude

Your strength and Your peace are enveloped around,
sanctified and justified my spirit is found

On my knees You direct my path and I begin to pray,
so, come precious Spirit in the cool of the day

Roman Road

I am the owner of the problem and its name is sin
I am damaged, unclean, and filthy from within

Condemned to death in a place called hell,
for this is the place made specifically for sinners to dwell

There is a price to be paid to ransom my soul
It will not be cheap to redeem me from Sheol

There is but One who is righteous and true,
only One I will accept in the place of you

Why would anyone do such a thing, I said?
Why would anyone go to his death in my stead?

He is My only Son and most precious to Me
He is the only worthy payment; it is how it must be

This is Our gift to the entire human race
The gift of eternal life by the Savior's grace

In my meager existence, I struggled to conceive,
the requirement is to accept him as Lord and believe

Believe that he is My Son and I raised him from the dead
Believe his spilled blood is the wine and broken body, the bread

This is a choice, you see, to believe in his name
In Our love for you, the reason he came

For it is in his name that you must confess
It is in his name that I will bless

When my mortal being understood the magnitude and passion of this gift, and that it was for me,
I said, yes Lord, I believe! I confessed, asked for forgiveness, and bowed each knee

The Calling

Revive in us, O God, a hunger for the lost
Put into perspective the blood You spilled, Your sacrifice, and cost

Send Your Holy Spirit to dwell among the saints,
breaking down all barriers and pushing through restraints

Empower our spirit to boldly pursue Your calling,
remembering those held captive within evil's enthralling

Let us see those the world has overlooked
Give us love and compassion; may our purpose never be mistook

Let the darkness retreat at home and abroad,
nor let the enemy obtain ground where Your laborers have trod

Saturate with love and hope the hardened hearts You have softened
Let us dwell in Your presence and speak of Your grace often

Rain joy and peace until it overflows
Help us reflect Your radiance in all gifts You have bestowed

As You prepare our spirit for warfare which will collide,
we shall have no fear, for in Your name all things must abide

Harvest

O, merciful Heavenly Father, I come to You in worship this new
    and glorious day
I bow before Your splendor and approach Your throne of grace

I thank You, Lord, for Your love and care, and all the blessings
    You have graciously bestowed
I thank You for the air I breathe and the beauties which You alone
    behold

In humility, I come to You that You may know my heart
Purify me and penetrate my thoughts and acts, setting me apart

If I harbor things, not of You, reveal them and help me to repent,
in so doing I will strive to emit Your attitudes and in holiness
    represent

With Your love and gentleness let me be patient and have
    self-control
Let me be good, kind, and faithful, with joy and peace console

It is by Your Spirit I await these grateful and expectant requests
It is within this atmosphere mountains will move and crumble,
    and to You that I attest

I praise You, Lord, and thank You for hearing me when I pray
I thank You, Lord, and in humbleness I lay this before You today

Paradise

The Master Craftsman diligently readies my rooms illuminated
    by affirmation
The Architect's perfection and attentiveness beyond any human
    imagination

My citizenship already secured and awaiting express passage
A paradise like no one on earth could either describe or relay by
    message

Upon the holy mountain, the citizens gather there
Names recorded in the Lamb's Book of Life and upon each heart
    declared

At the throne of grace, celestial harmonies transcend to our God
    and Lord
Thousands upon thousands joyfully worshiping in one accord

After awaiting instruction from Almighty God alerting Christ the
    time has come,
heaven opens and makes way for him to make war and of the
    judgment to be done

Beyond a millennium, the old had passed and the new emerged
    in descent,
out of the heavens the new Holy City spectacular and
    luminescent

God's people are there, and he dwells among them, and the lion
 lies down with the lamb
All tears, pain, and death are in the state of quondam

He who is seated on the throne has made everything new
He gives water to the thirsty from the spring of the Water of Life,
 his name Faithful and True

It is the place where the victorious inherit and reign with their
 God and King
Brilliant is the Holy City exquisitely as luminous as the crystal
 brings

The interior city made of impeccable gold, shines as clear glass,
its walls made of jasper and decorated with every precious stone;
 the radiance unsurpassed

The foundation is laid with the most precious jewels displayed in
 glorious splendor
The gates, all twelve, tower in wonder of pearl; the likes of which
 there is no contender

The city and its great street, pure gold; the gates—always open
 and no need of sun or moon,
for it is God himself who gives the light and Christ's lamp sacrifi-
 cially hewn

Within the border of the Heavenly City are the glory and honor
 of the nations
Impurity, deceitfulness, and shame have been exchanged by the
 spilling of Christ's libations

Flowing through the middle of the city runs the river of the Wa-
 ter of Life,
it flows directly from the throne of God and of the Lamb in
 whom all sustainment derives

On each side of the river stands the Tree of Life bearing twelve
    monthly fruits
Its leaves are for the healing of the nations and there are no more
    curses; of God are the attributes

The reward of citizenship in this Holy City is easy and sure—
invite the Lord Jesus into your heart as Lord of your life—John
    3:16 is not obscure

Quantify

In my quiet place, I sense tranquility of Your presence soft and sure
My hope and trust I place in You; by design, I am of Your contour

Regardless of on the mountain top or in the valley below,
I am absolute of Your nearness and seek communion to flow

When I reach a summit, there You are calling me higher,
but when I am lower than low, You are with me through the fire

Within this solace my thoughts take flight upon the gentle breeze
For in this place it is only You that I wish to please

What could I possibly give You that You don't already possess?
But then You remind me, until my last breath, it is *time*—and it is time I wish to invest

The Touch

The Master, coming here; is it true? How can it be true? But how could I ever get to him?
I suppose I could look upon his face as he walks by, possibly from the outer rim

Oh, but if I could only reach out and touch him, ever so lightly, who would even know?
If there is the slightest possibility, maybe a blessing he would bestow

Oh, so weary am I, and rapidly losing hope
This issue; the isolation and shunning; I am not sure how much longer I can cope

I must go, I must try; of course, I have to try
He is the Man of God, a healer, I must reach out and touch him as he goes by

Oh, there he is! But look at everyone crowding all around; this endeavor may prove too much
I will push through; come up from behind. All I need is the lightest touch

Out of desperation, I am reaching, reaching to be healed and remain discreet
It happened! It is a miracle; the healing is complete!

And then . . . he stopped. "*Who touched Me?*" he asked, but the
   answer was concealed
"*Power has gone out from Me.*" He knew someone had been
   healed

I trembled, for he was aware somebody reached out and touched
   his cloak
The crowd denying any touch, I fell at his feet, and then I spoke

I told him of my plight and how I had bled now these twelve
   years
I told him how no other could heal and was dismissed despite my
   tears

I told him my only hope was to touch him as he walked by—
and how I tried to be unassuming; but I knew I could not lie

I told him how I was instantly healed the moment his cloak was
   touched
I told him I knew I would be healed and needed only to reach out
   inasmuch

He said, "*Go in Peace, daughter; your faith has made you whole,*"
consumed by the Master's touch—in splendid wonder and praises
   to him did I extol

Peace Be Still

Snap goes the anchor, and the ground begins to shake
The safety net is torn, and surety begins to break

The sleeping dragon awakens, lifting his ugly head,
searching high and low for prey targeted by his dread

Silent is the wind that carries its breath below
Roaring hums of gatherings distant as next winter's snow

The whole earth watches as the dragon gains in force
Scholars left and right say we must stay the course

Uncertainty looming as economies threaten to collapse and fall
Taking root in this conception could be cataclysm for us all

F-e-a-r is this dragon, and he comes with many horns,
ready to pounce upon our peace, prickly with countless thorns

But, let me tell you of the one who says, *"Peace be still"*
The one whose light shines as a city on a hill

Though the ground may shutter, and we feel our fortress shake,
it is upon his foundation which he invites us to partake

Governments and economies, he set order in motion
He is the calm in the storm and to him we owe devotion

Resilient are the people he has created in love
In times of trouble, he is a very present help above

The Lord our God is absolute in his existence
He is searching every heart with loving, caring persistence

He is not the founder of this dragon called fear today,
although, he can use any method to keep us from going astray

If you knock, he is there answering to be sure
Jesus, the author and finisher of our faith; trust—and his assurance he will secure

Breathe

Ponderings of the year before pronounced the great eclipse
The year when sanguinity seemed beyond the grasping of her
    fingertips

Grief and pain suffocated life within her clouded sanctum
Fatigue and decline wreaked discord on her objective spectrum

Up from the deep, she looked upon Your grace
The weeping shadows of the wind gathered remembrance face

Like a rushing river driving fear from the west,
she could see the Lord's glory shining sure as the rising sun attests

She understood at times, he speaks in an all-consuming whisper
Captivating these thoughts, she was hopeful she would one day
    be better

Hopeful the gentle whisper of his breath would whisk her from
    the ailing wave
Hopeful the breath of God would rescue her from her depressing
    cave

She called upon the breath of God who breathes life into
    mankind
She called upon the breath of God for body, spirit, and of sound
    mind

The same breath that spoke when the heavens and its hosts were made
The only breath that in rebuke reveals how the world's foundations were laid

The breath which from his nostrils piled up the waters and displayed dry ground
Those same waters, when released, where all of Pharaoh's lifeless army was found

The breath that was breathed into man to give understanding
The very breath that breathed his Holy Spirit by his commanding

The breath that blew the water from the receding flood
The breath that from a cross exhaled and in the silence resounded his body's spilling blood

She thanked the living, breathing God for faith to believe her healing was to come
Meditating on the God-breathed Word, trusted she would rise and overcome

And There is Praise

Shall You tread on oceans wide or search throughout the land on high,
looking intently at every heart within every passer-by?

I am watching with discontent; quiet unrest pulling me by the hand,
wind blowing, thunder rolling but hollowness is on-demand

Deeply and powerfully the dream pulls me in
Paralyzed, frantic, and dismayed, I cannot find the fishers of men

Self-satisfaction is the norm—despisers of the good
They will not listen, they will not believe—oh if only they would!

In the darkness there I lay, watching out of my skin
I am helpless, immobile, waiting . . . waiting; in his time it will begin

Can you not see him in every morning and evening sky?
With every newborn child, how could you deny?

Dry bones walking consumed by their device,
searching for the latest, the greatest, whatever will entice

Where is the hope and where is the joy?
When You are mentioned most seem to be annoyed

The Sabbath came; at hand only one or two,
church parking lots mostly empty except for a few

What about salvation, forgiveness, and his peace?
Why is no one witnessing? For eternity there is no release!

I cannot move, I cannot shout nor praise his name,
as if I am bound and gagged, his name I cannot proclaim

Is the cunning one winning—
the ancient one cast down after time's beginning?

All his lies and deception claiming multitudes of souls
I am sickened and confused! Where are the ashes and the coal?

Then . . . ground shaking . . . earth flinging . . .
The rocks broke open and began singing!

Praise to our Lord and mighty King, they cried out!
Glory and honor to the Holy Lamb of God, they continued to
    shout!

Startled, I awoke and realized I had been dreaming
I shouted praises to God, then began thinking about this meaning

Lord, never let me take for granted the privilege of praising You!
May Your heart and mind be upon my life, in which I will pursue

Strength in the Light

Beyond the shadows are rays of light bringing promise in the new day
Once more, relentless, and deceitful threats attempt to make their way

I will not lose heart nor stifle the truth of that which is my calling
I am under no illusions: the enemy's threats are nothing but appalling

Reminders of my mistakes and faults, the devil would relish on instant replay,
for if he can keep me silent, he will mark it a victory, considering me his prey

My God is bigger than doubts seeking ransom of my joy,
for he is the one I love and serve; grace does he deploy

Through my weakness he makes me bold and strong
I am clay unearthed delighting in only his song

I can tell of the goodness, mercy, and compassion my Savior provides
Through Jesus, I am a conqueror bearing scars in which his blood was applied

Though wounded, not broken; confused but not forsaken,
in my Lord, I AM a force unshaken

The deceiver accuses and cunningly awaits my flesh to rise
I will choose not to take the bait and will hold out for him who is my prize

My eyes are open, and I know any power of my accuser is temporal, at best
Do not be dismayed by the evil one's tactics or the object of his quest

Trust in the one who wrote the Book and told us of its end
Put your faith in the great I AM and with him eternity you will spend

For His Purpose

In a higher realm, You dwell,
glories of all the universe You could tell

All riches, power, and authority are Yours alone,
for there is nothing to You that is unknown

And yet Your blood was spilled with me in mind,
not only for me but for all mankind

All things were created by Your mighty hand
Why You chose me, I'll never understand

Relationship and communion are Your desire
You rescued me and saved me from the muck and mire

I know to You I can express the troubles of my soul
Within my carnal understanding, the maladies of life take a toll

In all honesty, my spirit struggles with the reality of sickness and
  disease,
especially, knowing it is within Your power to remove it, as well
  as all pain relieve

It is the children for which I struggle the most,
for they could be healed by Your power and dominion through
  the Holy Ghost

However, it is not for me to question or in You to doubt
Help me have faith and trust You, Lord, from the inside out

For Your ways will never be known to man,
but we can be certain it is all for Your purpose and plan

Give us a peace surpassing all human comprehension
Hear our plea for all those in prayer we mention

Give the hurting and afflicted a touch from above
Let it be so, Lord, for those who are suffering, those who we love

Into Your throne room, we implore
Send us Your refreshing Spirit, Lord, forevermore

Growing

Thank You, Lord, for the rebuking that leads me closer to You
Thank You for the times of suffering and pain; it is only faith that brings me through

Why should You care for me so when each day I let You down?
I am so thankful You haven't given up on me; at Your feet I will one day lay my crown

Thank You also for all the love You've proven over and over, again
My thanks can never be enough for taking away my sin

As a bonus, You have allowed me to be a wife, a mother, and on down the line
Oh, those grandchildren; how my heart does pine!

Thank You for giving me a burden for the hurting and the lost
For all those brought to mind in prayer; it is not by chance our paths have crossed

Thank You for loving me through the worst versions of myself
For listening to me as I repent, or guiding my spirit if I attempt putting it on a shelf

Thank You for making the important things hard so they can be better appreciated
For relationships that are difficult, teaching me to love when it gets complicated

Thank You for making me aware when I am being critical and when I am judging
For reminding me the world is not fair; to rise above it instead of drudging

Thank You for the times I have been misjudged and even falsely accused
Thank You for letting me mature in You, no matter how I was confused

Thank You for making me stronger every time my faults are revealed
For correcting me over and over in lieu of keeping my faults concealed

I could go on and on about my shortcomings and how You have forgiven
Mostly, thank You for laying down Your life for mine and ultimately leading me to heaven

The Revelation

A trough for food and water is where my Savior lay
Though his glory seemingly without manifest that day

How the trough, symbolically and genuinely appropriate, this,
the Living Water and Bread of Life displayed here, within this
    premises

The Glory of Heaven proclaimed amidst a remote shepherd's field
The Good News of this joy, to the world, seemingly concealed

A light of revelation and the Bright Morning Star, to Your people,
    scribed and forecasted
Opposition followed him throughout his thirty-three years and
    outlasted

Wounds would mar his hands and feet and pierce the heart of his
    mother
The Passover Lamb to be led to slaughter, all in love for his
    brother

But not the end of his life, though he was, and is, and is to come
The second coming, divinity incarnate, proving his life no
    simulacrum

And when heaven stands open and the clouds unfold—
His image "The Lion of Judah"—an unimaginable sight to behold

Majestically seated on his white horse, its rider Faithful and True,
at such a time, the deity of Christ, at this who could argue?

Flames of fire penetrating his eyes and out of his mouth a striking sword
In righteousness, he judges and makes war within his own accord

Upon his head are many crowns and appellations which only to himself are known
His robe carries the blood of all martyrs and of those for whom he has atoned

No longer the image of the slaughtered Lamb laying down his life in love,
but the furious wrath of God, righteously judging, striking down nations of rebellion from above

With just a breath the wicked are crushed by the Word of God
While thunder peels and winds rage, the light of heaven descending as if many a lightning rod

There, the Revelation of Christ and his horse stand at the ready— his bride closely behind
The whole earth trembles and the heavens shake in the presence of all mankind

And as the saints await in faith, we cry out "Come, Lord Jesus, Come," upon Your name we call!
Upon his robe and upon his thigh appear, "King of kings and Lord of lords," in view of one and all.

Appendix

Scripture References and Inspirational Scripture

Alpha and Omega

Beginning—
Day 1: Line 1—Genesis 1:1
       Line 2—Genesis 1:2
       Line 3—Genesis 1:3
       Line 4—Genesis 1:4–5
Day 2: Line 5—Genesis 1:8
Day 3: Line 6—Genesis 1:10–11
Day 4: Line 7—Genesis 1:14–19
Day 5: Line 8—Genesis 1:20–26
Day 6: Line 9—Genesis 1:26
       Lines 10, 11—Genesis 1:27
       Line 12—Galatians 5:13
       Line 13—Genesis 3:6; Ezekiel 22:30; 1 Corinthians 15:45
       Line 14—Genesis 3:8–19
       Line 15—Luke 1:30–32; Hebrews 9:23–25
       Line 16—First Timothy 2:5–6
       Line 17—John 3:16; Ephesians 4:32
       Line 18—Mark 8:38; Romans 10:9; Colossians 1:10

Appendix

Line 19—John 11: 46-50
Line 20—John 11: 49-53
Line 21—John 18:12—19:37
Line 22—Psalm 118:22; Acts 4:11; Ephesians 2:20
Line 23—John 3:35-36
End— Line 24—Revelation 22:13, 20-21

What Was it Like

Line 1—Isaiah 53:6; Habakkuk 1:13; Matthew 27:46
Line 2—Isaiah 53:5; 1 Peter 2:24, 3:18
Line 3—Romans 3:23, 8:3
Line 4—Mark 15:16-32
Line 5—John 19:28-30
Line 6—Romans 16:20; Hebrews 2:14
Line 8—Matthew 27:51; Mark 15:38; Luke 23:45
Line 9—Matthew 20:28; Hebrews 7:26-27, 9:26; Revelation 1:5
Line 10—Romans 5:17; 1 Corinthians 15:3-4; Hebrews 10:12
Line 11—Psalm 103:12
Line 12—Romans 6:17-18
Line 13—Micah 7:19
Line 15—Ephesians 2:8-9
Line 16—Zechariah 12:10; John 14:6
Line 17—Ephesians 4:9; Revelation 1:18
Line 19—Luke 4:34-35
Line 20—Mark 5:7
Line 21—Luke 2:13
Line 24—First John 5:11

Amaze

Line 1—Romans 5:8
Line 2—Psalm 103:8
Line 3—Psalm 33:20, 62:5
Line 4—Deuteronomy 31:6; Jude 1:20-21

Scripture References and Inspirational Scripture

Line 5—Exodus 14:14; Isaiah 52:12
Line 6—Hebrews 4:13
Line 11—Deuteronomy 6:5; Matthew 22:37-39
Line 12—Deuteronomy 11:27
Line 13—First John 4:8, 16
Line 14—John 13:34-35; 1 John 4:7-12
Line 15—Isaiah 14:24
Line 16—Psalm 46:10
Line 17—Hebrews 4:12
Line 18—Psalm 103:8
Line 19—Psalm 37:7
Line 20—Romans 8:38-39
Line 21—Psalm 62:7; 1 Corinthians 6:20
Line 22—Psalm 79:13; Lamentations 5:19
Line 23—Psalm 78:13
Line 24—Psalm 8:4, 84:11; Hebrews 4:16; 1 Peter 5:7
Line 25—Titus 2:13-14

The Armor of God

Lines 1, 2—Isaiah 54:17; Ephesians 6:11, 13, 16
Line 3—First Corinthians 15:57; Hebrews 4:16
Line 4—Psalm 103:19; Proverbs 3:26; Colossians 1:16-17
Line 5—John 10:10; 1 Peter 5:8
Line 6—Psalm 62:6
Line 7—Matthew 28:18; Philippians 2:9
Line 8—John 5:30; Ephesians 6:10
Lines 9, 10—Ephesians 6:11-18
Lines 11, 12—Ephesians 6:14
Line 13—Ephesians 6:15
Line 14—Romans 12:12; Ephesians 6:18; 1 Thessalonians 5:17
Line 15—Ephesians 6:17
Line 16—First Peter 2:9
Lines 17, 18—Proverbs 30:5; Ephesians 6:17
Line 19—Second Timothy 2:3

Appendix

Line 20—Ephesians 6:13
Line 21—Second Corinthians 10:5
Line 22—Psalm 25:21
Line 23—Ephesians 6:11
Line 24—Genesis 3:1-5
Line 25—Matthew 6:10; Ephesians 2:8
Line 26—Psalm 66:2, 69:34; Romans 8:26; 2 Corinthians 1:20

Battle Cry of an Overcomer

Line 17—John 10:10
Lines 19, 20—Psalm 109:2; Proverbs 15:28
Line 24—Psalm 46:1
Line 30—John 16:33
Line 31—Joshua 1:5
Line 32—Psalm 46:10
Line 35—Psalm 37:18
Line 37—Psalm 109:3
Line 38—Matthew 27:38
Line 39—Matthew 5:44
Line 40—First Peter 2:15
Line 42—Psalm 119:105
Line 44—First Peter 5:10
Line 45—Second Corinthians 2:11
Line 46—Hosea 1:10
Line 47—Psalm 91:4
Line 48—Psalm 105:2
Line 49—Genesis 50:20; James 1:12
Line 51—Ephesians 6:14-18
Line 53—First Chronicles 16:11
Line 54—John 8:32
Line 56—Jude 1:25

Scripture References and Inspirational Scripture

Refinement

Line 1—Psalm 145:18
Line 2—James 1:2
Line 3—James 1:3-4
Lines 4, 5—James 1:5
Line 6—Proverbs 3:6
Line 7—Psalm 86:15, 141:3; James 3:5-10
Line 8—Psalm 24:5-6; Proverbs 8:13
Line 9—Psalm 37:7
Line 10—Psalm 90:17
Line 11—Psalm 120:1
Line 12—Psalm 18:6; Matthew 7:7-8
Line 13—Galatians 6:2; James 1:21
Line 14—Psalm 5:12; Romans 5:9
Line 15—Psalm 143:10
Line 16—Second Corinthians 12:10
Line 17—Psalm 27:1
Line 18—Isaiah 41:13
Line 19—Romans 8:28
Line 20—Hebrews 11:1-12
Line 21—Psalm 130:4
Line 22—Mark 4:3-8
Line 23—Psalm 61:2
Line 24—Proverbs 25:4

A Day at the Beach

Line 1—Psalm 96:11; Colossians 1:17
Line 6—Philippians 4:7; 2 Thessalonians 3:16
Line 20—Psalm 46:10; Proverbs 3:5-6; Colossians 3:2

Appendix

Burgundy

Line 1—First Peter 1:18–19
Line 3—Matthew 26:4, 27:1
Line 4—Mark 15:15, 24; John 19:34
Line 6—James 1:14–15
Line 8—First Corinthians 1:21
Line 9—Mark 15:15; John 17:1–5
Line 10—Ephesians 2:13; Colossians 1:20; 1 John 1:7
Line 11—Luke 23:34
Lines 12, 13—Mark 15:14–15
Line 14—First Timothy 2:6
Line 15—Hebrews 9:28
Line 16—Hebrews 2:14–18
Line 17—Exodus 25:17–22; Romans 3:23–25
Line 18—Second Corinthians 5:19
Line 19—John 15:13
Line 20—First Peter 2:24
Line 21—John 3:16; Romans 5:11, 18
Line 22—Ephesians 1:7; Romans 3:25, 5:19–21

Intentional Devotion

Line 1—Joshua 4:24; Psalm 100:3
Line 2—Isaiah 50:4
Line 3—Second Thessalonians 3:3
Line 4—Psalm 73:28
Line 5—Isaiah 11:2–3
Line 6—Romans 12:2
Line 7—James 1:5
Line 8—Joshua 1:9; 1 Corinthians 16:13
Line 9—Psalm 55:22
Line 10—Ephesians 4:32; Galatians 6:2
Line 11—First Timothy 2:4; 2 Timothy 2:24–25; Titus 1:1–2
Line 12—Psalm 9:9, 82:3, 103:6

Scripture References and Inspirational Scripture

Posterity

Title—Preamble to the Constitution
Line 3—Preamble to the Constitution
Line 4—Preamble to the Constitution
Line 5—M. L. King Jr's "I Have a Dream" speech
Line 13—Colonial Flag
Line 14—Subsequent flags
Line 19—Revolutionary War
Line 23—"Gettysburg Address"
Line 24—Civil War
Line 31—"America the Beautiful"
Line 32—"America the Beautiful"
Line 35—"Star-Spangled Banner;" American currency
Line 36—"The Pledge of Allegiance"

Under His Wing

Lines 1, 2, 3, 4—First Peter 5:8
Lines 5, 6—Second Corinthians 2:11
Line 7—John 8:44
Line 11—Genesis 3:1
Line 12—Ephesians 6:10–18
Line 14—John 10:10
Line 16—Romans 14:11
Line 17—John 17:15
Line 18—Second Samuel 22:17–20
Line 19—Second Corinthians 4:8–9
Line 20—Romans 16:20
Line 21—James 1:2–4
Line 23—Psalm 23:3; Isaiah 40:31; 1 Peter 5:10–11
Line 25—Matthew 28:18
Line 26—Psalm 63:7
Line 27—Second Corinthians 4:8–9
Line 28—James 2:19

Appendix

The Cool of the Day

Line 1—Genesis 3:8
Line 2—Philippians 4:6; Revelation 3:20
Line 3—Psalm 43:3; Proverbs 1:5
Line 4—Psalm 86:11; 1 Corinthians 7:31
Line 5—Isaiah 32:18
Line 6—Hebrews 12:1; 1 Peter 5:7
Line 7—Proverbs 3:5-8
Line 8—Psalm 23:5; Luke 13:29,14:15
Line 9—Isaiah 40:29; Philippians 4:7
Line 10—Romans 8:30; Hebrews 10:14
Line 11—Psalm 119:35
Line 12—Job 33:4

Roman Road

Line 1—Romans 3:23
Line 2—Romans 3:16
Line 3—Psalm 16:10; John 5:29
Line 4—Luke 16:19-24; Revelation 21:8
Line 5—Romans 6:23
Line 6—Isaiah 53:10; John 19:1-4, 6-7, 15-24
Line 7—Romans 3:11-12; 2 Corinthians 5:21
Line 8—Isaiah 53:11-12; John 3:16
Line 9—John 17:3
Line 10—John 17:24-26
Line 11—Acts 2:22-23
Line 12—John 1:14
Lines 13, 14—John 1:9-13
Line 16—John 12:44; Romans 10:13-15
Line 17—Romans 10:9
Line 18—Matthew 26:26-28
Line 19—Matthew 18:3, 23:37
Line 20—Romans 5:8

Scripture References and Inspirational Scripture

Line 21—Philippians 2:8-11
Line 22—First John 4:9
Line 23—Hebrews 11:3-6, 12:2
Line 24—John 1:9; Romans 14:11; Philippians 2:10-11

The Calling

Line 1—Luke 19:10
Line 2—Luke 22:44; Mark 15:25
Line 3—John 14:26
Line 4—Second Thessalonians 2:7
Line 5—Mark 16:15
Line 6—Second Timothy 2:26
Line 7—Job 5:15-16; Proverbs 31:8-9
Line 8—Deuteronomy 15:7
Line 9—Mark 1:23-26
Line 10—Matthew 28:19-20; Luke 4:43
Line 11—First Timothy 1:14-15
Line 12—Ephesians 2:8-9
Line 13—Romans 15:13
Line 14—First Corinthians 12:8-10
Line 15—Ephesians 6:12
Line 16—Isaiah 41:10

Harvest

Line 1—Psalm 100:2
Line 2—Psalm 95:6; Hebrews 4:16
Line 3—Nahum 1:7; 1 Peter 5:7
Line 4—Psalm 50:2; Colossians 2:6-7
Line 5—Proverbs 22:4
Line 6—Proverbs 11:2; Philippians 2:1-2
Line 7—Jeremiah 4:14
Line 8—Psalm 93:5
Lines 9, 10—Galatians 5:22-23; Colossians 3:12

Appendix

Line 11—Psalm 4:1; Philippians 4:6
Line 12—Psalm 17:6
Line 13—First John 5:14
Line 14—Psalm 55:22

Paradise

Lines 1, 2—John 14:2
Line 3—Philippians 3:20
Line 4—Luke 23:43
Line 5—Hebrews 12:22
Line 6—Hebrews 12:23; Revelation 13:8
Lines 7, 8—Job 38:7; Hebrews 12:22
Line 9—Mark 13:32-37
Line 10—Revelation 19:11
Lines 11, 12, 13, 14, 15—Isaiah 11:6; Revelation 5:5-6, 21:1-5
Line 16—John 7:38; Revelation 19:11, 21:6
Line 17—Second Timothy 2:12; Revelation 21:7
Line 18—Revelation 21:11
Lines 19, 20, 21, 22—Revelation 21:18-21
Line 23—Revelation 21:21, 23, 25
Line 24—Revelation 21:23
Line 25—Revelation 21:26
Line 26—Revelation 21:27
Lines 27, 28—Revelation 22:1-2
Lines 29, 30—Revelation 22:2
Lines 31, 32—John 3:16

Quantify

Line 1—Psalm 91:1
Line 2—Psalm 71:5; Acts 17:29
Line 3—Psalm 23:4, 43:3
Line 4—Deuteronomy 4:7; Psalm 75:1
Line 5—Psalm 61:2

Scripture References and Inspirational Scripture

Line 6—Psalm 141:1
Line 7—Job 32:8
Line 8—Second Corinthians 5:9
Line 9—Deuteronomy 10:14; Psalm 24:1
Line 10—Luke 12:8, 21

The Touch

Luke 8:42-48

Peace Be Still

Line 13—Mark 4:39
Line 14—Matthew 5:14
Line 16—Luke 6:48
Line 17—Romans 13:1
Line 18—Psalm 107:29
Line 20—Psalm 46:1
Line 21—John 1:1
Line 22—John 3:16
Line 25—Matthew 7:7
Line 26—Hebrews 12:2

Breathe

Line 5—Psalm 51:1; Hebrews 4:16
Line 7—Isaiah 59:19
Line 8—Psalm 50:1, 104:31
Line 9—First Kings 19:12; Job 26:14
Line 10—Romans 12:2; 2 Corinthians 10:5
Line 11—Ezekiel 37:12-14
Line 12—Job 33:4
Line 13—Genesis 2:7
Line 14—Romans 12:2; 1 Thessalonians 5:23; 2 Timothy 1:7

Appendix

Line 15—Psalm 33:6
Line 16—Second Samuel 22:16; Psalm 18:7-8, 15
Line 17—Exodus 15:8
Line 18—Exodus 15:10
Line 19—Job 32:8
Line 20—John 20:22
Line 21—Genesis 8:1
Line 22—Mark 15:37
Line 23—Job 33:4; Mark 9:24; Hebrews 11:1
Line 24—Second Timothy 3:16; Hebrews 4:12

And There is Praise

Line 2—Second Corinthians 4:18
Line 6—Matthew 4:19
Line 7—Romans 3:18
Line 8—Matthew 13:58
Line 11—Genesis 1:31; Psalm 50:1; Ecclesiastes 1:5
Line 12—Job 31:15
Line 19—Matthew 6:14; John 3:16; Philippians 4:7
Line 24—Isaiah 14:12
Line 25—John 8:44
Line 26—Job 42:6; Isaiah 6:6-7; Ezekiel 27:30
Line 28—Luke 19:40

Strength in the Light

Line 1—Lamentations 3:22-23
Line 2—Psalm 31:20
Line 3—John 15:16
Line 4—John 10:10
Line 5—Ephesians 6:11-12; Revelation 12:10
Line 6—First Peter 5:8
Line 7—John 15:11
Lines 8, 9—Second Corinthians 12:9-10

Scripture References and Inspirational Scripture

Line 10—Psalm 145:7; Isaiah 64:8
Line 11—Exodus 33:19; Psalm 69:16, 86:16
Line 12—Romans 8:37–39
Line 13—Second Corinthians 4:8–9
Line 14—Romans 3:25–26; Hebrews 12:27–28
Line 15—Galatians 5:24
Line 16—Romans 8:13
Lines 17, 18—First Peter 5:8–9; Revelation 12:10
Line 19—Revelation 12:11, 22:16
Line 20—Ecclesiastes 3:11; John 3:15–16; Ephesians 2:8–9

For His Purpose

Line 1—Psalm 113:5
Line 2—Genesis 1:14–18; Psalm 19:1
Line 3—Job 26:14, 42:2
Line 4—Hebrews 4:13
Line 5—Matthew 26:27–28
Line 6—First Timothy 2:3–6
Line 7—Jeremiah 32:17; Revelation 1:8
Line 8—Matthew 18:12–13
Line 9—First John 4:9–10
Line 10—First Corinthians 6:11; 1 Timothy 1:15
Line 11—Philippians 4:6
Line 12—Job 22:10–11; John 16:33
Line 13—Mark 5:25–26
Line 14—Isaiah 53:5
Line 15—Luke 8:41–42
Line 16—First Corinthians 12:9
Line 17—Proverbs 3:5; Isaiah 26:4
Line 18—Psalm 115:11; Jeremiah 17:7
Line 19—Isaiah 55:8
Line 20—Romans 8:28; Ephesians 3:11
Line 21—Ephesians 3:19
Line 22—Psalm 72:12

Appendix

Line 23—Psalm 140:12
Line 24—Psalm 9:18
Line 25—Hebrews 4:16; Revelation 4:1-11
Line 26—Acts 3:20

Growing

Line 1—Proverbs 3:12; Hebrews 12:6
Line 2—Isaiah 48:10; 2 Corinthians 1:3-5
Line 3—Romans 3:23
Line 4—Romans 3:24; 2 Corinthians 12:9-10; 1 Peter 5:4
Line 5—Psalm 136:1; 1 John 4:10
Line 6—Matthew 26:28; John 1:29
Lines 7, 8—Psalm 127:3-5
Lines 9, 10—Psalm 34:18; Galatians 6:2
Line 11—Psalm 36:5
Line 12—Psalm 119:59-60; Acts 2:38
Line 13—First Thessalonians 5:18
Line 14—Luke 6:27-28, 35-36
Line 15—Matthew 7:1; Romans 14:4; James 2:13, 4:11-12
Line 16—Philippians 1:29; 2 Timothy 1:7
Line 17—Psalm 35:20; Ephesians 6:12
Line 18—Proverbs 3:5-8; 1 Corinthians 14:33
Lines 19, 20—Psalm 19:12-13
Line 21—Ephesians 1:7, 2:4-5
Line 22—John 14:6; Colossians 1:22; Hebrews 10:10

The Revelation

Line 1—Luke 2:12
Line 2—Luke 2:17
Line 3—Luke 2:12, 10:21
Line 4—John 4:10-11, 6:35
Line 5—Luke 2:9, 13
Line 6—Luke 2:10

Scripture References and Inspirational Scripture

Line 7—Luke 2:32; Revelation 22:16
Line 8—John 15:19-21
Line 9—Luke 2:34-35
Line 10—Isaiah 53:7-12; John 10:11
Line 11—Revelation 1:8
Line 12—Isaiah 40:21-26
Line 13—Revelation 19:11
Line 14—Revelation 5:5, 19:12-13
Line 15—Revelation 19:11
Line 16—John 17:1-5
Line 17—Revelation 19:12, 15
Line 18—Revelation 19:11
Line 19—Revelation 19:12
Line 20—Romans 5:8; Revelation 19:13
Line 21—Isaiah 53:7
Line 22—Revelation 19:15
Line 23—Revelation 19:13
Line 24—Psalm 77:17-19
Line 25—Revelation 19:11, 14
Line 26—Psalm 77:18; Hebrews 12:26; Revelation 19:11-15
Line 27—Revelation 22:21
Line 28—Revelation 19:16

Bibliography

Bellamy, Francis. 1971. *The Pledge of allegiance.* Art Evans Productions.
Fisher, William Arms, and Katharine Lee Bates. "America the Beautiful." Oliver Ditson Company, Boston MA, 1917. Noted Music.
King, Martin L., Jr. "I Have a Dream." Speech presented at the March on Washington for Jobs and Freedom, Washington, DC, August 1963.
Lincoln, Abraham. "Gettysburg Address." Speech, Gettysburg, PA, November 19, 1863. "American Speeches", National Archives. Accessed April 13, 2021. https://bit.ly/3a9JR5V.
Smith, John Stafford, and Francis Scott Key. "Star Spangled Banner." Oliver Ditson, 1918. Noted Music.

www.ingramcontent.com/pod-product-compliance
Lightning Source LLC
Chambersburg PA
CBHW071745040426
42446CB00012B/2477